Taking It To The STREETS

Taking It To The STREETS

TED HAGGARD

WAGNER
PUBLICATIONS

Taking It to the Streets
Copyright © 2002
by Ted Haggard
ISBN 1-58502-024-9

Published by
Wagner Publications
11005 N. Highway 83
Colorado Springs, CO 80921
www.wagnerpublications.org

Cover design by
Imagestudios
100 East St. Suite 105
Colorado Springs, CO 80903
719-578-0351

Edited by
Rebecca Sytsema

Interior design by
Rebecca Sytsema

Rights for publishing this book in other languages are contracted by Gospel Literature International (GLINT). GLINT also provides technical help for the adaptation, translation, and publishing of Bible study resources and books in scores of languages worldwide. For further information, contact GLINT, P.O. Box 4060, Ontario, CA 91761-1003, USA. You may also send e-mail to glintint@aol.com, or visit their web site at www.glint.org.

1 2 3 4 5 6 7 8 9   08 07 06 05 04 03 02

Contents

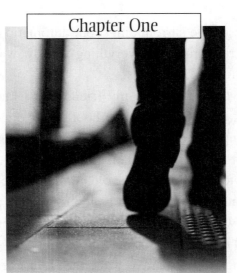

Chapter One

Meeting Your City
with Engaging
Prayers

Pentagrams, ankhs, and bloodied, swollen faces were painted on the walls and ceiling of the old drainage system where we were walking. The beams from our flashlights barely dispelled the darkness as we inched our way through the maze of tunnels, pipes, and caves that crisscrossed the abandoned mining zone. What was once a bustle of mining activity was now a home for satanic worship. For several hours, we tromped carefully through the meandering ruins, praying in hushed voices one moment, calling out powerful praise the next. It was nearly impossible not to stay focused—

in these desperate surroundings, our automatic reflex was to pray desperate prayers. Everything we saw was motivation to call out to the Lord Jesus.

Earlier that afternoon, my friend and I had decided to prayerwalk one of the neighborhoods near our homes. But we had bumped into a police officer and talked with him about the most problematic and dangerous places in town, and he directed us to these ruins of the old mining district in Colorado Springs that were an obvious hangout for dark powers. We were glad we had come—there was little doubt that no one had prayed for this area in years, if ever.

Not long after our prayerwalk, the city forced the owners to clean it up. As the grotesque images were removed from the walls, so was one of the dominant negative spiritual strongholds in our city. It was no longer dark and foreboding, no longer an invitation for violent activity, so the violent activity there stopped.

This is why I love the adventure of prayerwalking, or walking through an area while interceding for that place. The churches in Colorado Springs have been doing it for years now, and every time we go, something good happens that improves our community. Steady streams of miracles seem to accompany prayerwalking, and it's not difficult to figure out why.

MOVING, FEELING, AND SEEING: IT WORKS BETTER

Praying while walking makes prayer purposeful, informed, and stimulated for a variety of reasons, the first of which is physical. Walking keeps our bodies moving and helps us to stay alert—it's difficult to fall asleep praying when you're crossing a busy intersection downtown. In fact, I usually walk around or pace even during my daily personal prayer time. I love to sit and quietly pray to God or kneel to worship Him, but more often than not, I find that my prayers are more intentional and focused if I keep my body moving. It simply keeps my mind from wandering.

In addition, there is a great difference between praying for a community from your prayer closet and praying for a community while walking through it. Both are valuable, but prayerwalking lets you see the sights, hear the sounds, and smell the smells of the community, giving you constant ideas about how to pray for people.

When you're seeing and feeling the places and the people you're praying for, you are more apt to pray specifically and fervently.

> Prayerwalking is a vital tool we can use to change the world. It is a way of making certain that everyone in my city has someone standing in the gap for them and interceding on their behalf.

I have been on prayerwalks in Europe, the Middle East, Asia, and Africa. Though I had prayed for the people who live in those places for years, something special happened to my faith when I was actually there. Seeing the pagan sacrifices, watching the blood flow, and seeing parents drag their children to these horrible ceremonies made me keenly aware of the spiritual climate around me. And it made a difference in how I prayed.

This same insight is true of your own neighborhood. I have often gone to a local park or schoolyard where I would sit on the curb and pray for the playing children. Seeing them reminds me to pray for their moms and dads, teachers and administrators, brothers and sisters. Most of all, I pray that God's perfect plan for their lives will be accomplished. Seeing them reminds me that they really live and breathe—*there they are right in front of me*—and that each one has an eternal destiny. That knowledge motivates me to pray more specifically and passionately.

Deuteronomy 11:22-25 describes what we want for our cities. It reads, "If you carefully observe all these commands I am giving you to follow—to love the Lord your God, to walk in all his ways and to hold fast to him—then the Lord will drive out all these nations before you and you will dispossess nations larger and stronger than you. *Every place where you set your foot will be yours...no man will be able to stand against you.* The Lord your God, as he promised you, will put the terror and fear of you on the whole land, wherever you go" (emphasis mine).

We use this Scripture as a type, or representation, of what God longs to do today. God was promising the Israelites that He would drive out wicked influences and strongholds. For today, this is His promise—that if we will obey His word and physically walk over the land, we can dispossess nations. That means we can beat back the forces that create darkness in people's hearts. If we are faithful to the Lord and willing to call on His name for our land, we will be victorious in hindering negative spiritual activity—the type of activity that promotes alcoholism, sexual sin, resentfulness, bitterness, and rebellion. We are the church, and God has granted us the power and opportunity to change the world for Him.

Prayerwalking is a vital tool we can use to change the world. It is a tool I use to make the light of God brighter in my community. It is a way of making certain that everyone in my city has someone standing in the gap for them and interceding on their behalf.

ENGAGING PRAYER: COMMUNION AND CONFRONTATION

When we pray we do two things: commune with God and confront demonic schemes. Communion is the most important thing we do, so about 95% of my prayer time is focused on Christ and His Word. Fellowship with the Holy Spirit is my greatest joy. It establishes the purpose of my life. Sharing in His purpose is the reason we all exist. However, for us to enjoy full freedom in our communion with God, we also have to know how to confront demonic schemes. Because Christ is so powerful, it usually only takes 5% or less of my prayer time, but it is vitally important in successfully advancing His kingdom.

I call genuine spiritual communion and confrontation "engaging prayer." In order to pray effectively, we must both successfully engage the Spirit of God and challenge and defeat demonic powers. We must commune *and* confront.

Communing with God is not reciting Christian phrases and saying nice things to God hoping that He hears us.

Genuine communion requires His Spirit and our spirit to touch, intermingle, fellowship, and become one. Real communion is not our intellect speaking to His, and vise versa. It's heart to heart—His Spirit and our spirit becoming one. When this happens, God's dreams and visions flood into our spirit and we are able to pray prayers with faith because they are actually directed by the Holy Spirit. At this point, there is no power that can stop our prayers from being answered. When we commune with God, He prepares us for war.

But confrontation is not just rebuking, binding, preventing, or shouting at demonic forces and demanding that they leave. It is our spirit praying from the position of Christ Himself and actually representing Him in engaging demonic powers and neutralizing them. It is both intelligent—understanding our position in Christ—and spiritual—discerning unseen realities. Engaging prayer is confrontational and powerful, and it always produces tangible results.

ENERGIZING YOUR PRAYER LIFE

Because genuine prayer requires engaging the Holy Spirit for communion and the powers of darkness for confrontation, it is important that we stay alert. Too often when we pray we are distracted with thoughts about pressing issues, projects, or problems. But as millions of intercessors have found, walking, pacing, rocking, kneeling, bowing, lifting hands, and other physical movements help us express our prayers.

In my regular times of prayer at church or at home, I enjoy praying over maps of the city, the names of people who attend our church, other pastors and churches in the city, government officials, and family members. But if I do all of this in one room, things that need to be done and the pressure of time often distract me from the work of prayer. When distractions become consuming, I'll often leave the room and go on a prayerwalk. While walking and praying through the city, the sights and activities of the community give me fresh prayer ideas and make it possible to focus on His plan once again.

Another problem in prayer is boredom. If you grew up in a church like the one I grew up in, the mental images of prayer are very disheartening. Sitting in a circle holding hands with people for extended periods of time can put me to sleep faster than the most potent Nyquil. Although some people can sit still and focus at length on one or two specific items for prayer, I was not graced with this ability.

If I am praying in a room, I like to pace. If I'm sitting in a chair, I usually gently rock back and forth. If there is privacy and the Lord seems to be speaking to me, I will often lie down on the floor and listen. But even then, if I want to spend time with Him for an extended period, getting outside and praying over the community keeps my mind on the purpose of my prayers: knowing Him and blessing people.

PRAYERWALKING HELPS US CONNECT WITH PEOPLE

A few summers ago my friend Mark Marble and I rented a room in downtown Colorado Springs to fast and pray for a few days. From our room we could easily walk through the downtown area, pray discreetly, then return to the hotel to rest and talk (by the way, fasting and praying with a friend or two is a wonderful way to connect!).

On one of the evenings, we stayed out well after midnight praying through the streets. About 1:30 a.m. we were walking over a bridge and heard the cracking of skateboards and voices underneath. We stopped, peered over the edge and saw a group of teenagers playing around. Not wanting to pass up an opportunity for fun, we decided to scare them a little bit. I leaned over the top of the bridge and yelled down at them in a deep strong voice, "Hey you boys! What do you think you're doing down there?!"

They jumped and fearfully looked up at the silhouettes of two men leaning over the bridge glaring down at them. After a moment of thick silence, one of them timidly called out, "Pastor Ted, is that you?"

Boy, did I feel dumb! I looked around and tried to think of a reasonable explanation of why I was downtown in the middle of the night. Unable to come up with an excuse, I yelled back, "Uh, yes, it's me. Who are you?"

After hearing his name and learning that he and his family attended our church, Mark and I went down below to talk with the group of young men who had slipped out of their homes to skateboard under the bridge on a warm summer night.

Coincidence? I don't think so. That night this young man and his family became special to me. Over the following weeks we created a personal bond as we had some great laughs at church telling our story. Then a tragedy struck the family when the boy's mother died. I was asked to help conduct the funeral, and because of the encounter under the bridge, this family was not just one more family from the community, nor was I just the pastor asked to participate in the funeral. Because of prayerwalking, I was linked to this family in a special way that helped all of us deal with the departure of their mom.

WHAT ABOUT JESUS' WARNING?

During the Sermon on the Mount, Jesus said, "And when you pray, do not be like the hypocrites, for they love to pray standing in the synagogues and on the street corners to be seen by men. I tell you the truth, they have received their reward in full. But when you pray, go into your room, close the door and pray to your Father, who is unseen. Then your Father, who sees what is done in secret, will reward you" (Matthew 6:5-6).

Here, Jesus is concerned about those who pray in order to be seen praying. But prayerwalking is the opposite of praying publicly for vanity's sake. When you're prayerwalking, you are the only one who should know that you are praying. If you go with a friend, make it look like the two of you are just conversing as you walk. This way you can take turns leading each other in prayer. (I like to go with friends so we can pray for a while, talk for a while, pray for a while, and talk for a while. This can be fun, spiritually effective, discrete, and good for you spiritually and physically.) But whether you go with friends or alone, remember to be quiet and discrete.

Many of you reading this have probably prayerwalked before. Some of you may have never tried it or even heard of it. Either way, I want this book to encourage you and to help you understand the "why" and "how" of intercessory prayer. Prayer is simple, fun and—most importantly—imperative to increasing God's kingdom on the earth, and it's always good for us to learn how to pray more effectively. Once you've read this book, you'll know how to pray with insight and courage like never before.

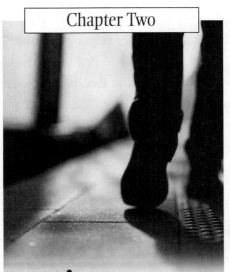

Chapter Two

Detecting
the
Spiritual Signs

Of course, the main reason prayerwalking helps your prayers be specific is that you see specific things to pray for—that is, you learn about the community as you walk through it, and you use that knowledge to guide your prayers. When you're walking, you may notice a Masonic image above the door of the county courthouse, and you'll know that the Masons were or are affiliated with that building. If you notice a pink triangle sign hanging in a churchyard, you know that church embraces homosexual practice, or that it is embracing an ultra-liberal interpretation of Scripture. Perhaps you'll see gang members in a courtyard or park. If so, you'll know to pray that God would silence and heal the gang element in that part of town.

As you pray through a neighborhood you may notice signs of poverty—dilapidated cars, homes in disrepair, vacant business buildings, etc. Pray for God to give the people better ideas and greater opportunities in earning a living. If you see obvious signs of wealth, you can pray that those resources will be used for God's kingdom. Wherever you go, closely observe the community as you prayerwalk. Try to become informed about the community in which you are praying.

> Using a spiritual map of the territory you are prayerwalking, you will be better informed about how to pray. You can make your prayer effort strategic, targeting [specific] parts of the city.

While we were praying for a small town once, we noticed that all of the churches looked like they had been built in the 1930s and 1940s. After researching the history of that community, we learned that the town had experienced a revival sixty years ago, but nothing much had happened since that time. We also learned that church attendance had been declining. These clues gave us understanding, so we were equipped to pray in a very specific manner for that town.

When you prayerwalk, keep your head up for these types of spiritual indicators. Be alert to the climate of the community. When you notice things that indicate a certain lifestyle or belief system, pray along those lines.

Just stepping outside your door and walking will help your prayers be specific; but with a little preparation, you can look even deeper into your community or prayerwalking target. There are three main ways the people in our church typically prepare for prayerwalks: drawing a spiritual map, grid praying, and keeping a general list of the types of strategic places to pray for.

SPIRITUAL MAPS

Spiritual maps work in much the same way as political or topographical maps. But instead of highlighting geographical facts, spiritual maps highlight spiritual facts. For example, while a political map delineates the borders between the United States and Mexico and shows the location of Paris in relation to London, a spiritual map details areas where the gospel has had an effect versus areas where there is no Christian influence.

One idea for using spiritual maps on a global scale is to take a map of the world and use blue shading to color all the countries where less than one percent of the people confess Christ as Lord. Then, you could use red to shade in the countries where one to five percent of the people know Christ. Countries where five to ten percent of the people confess Christ could be green, and yellow shading could designate those countries where more than ten percent of the people know Christ. As you pray for the nations at home or while actually visiting them, the color scheme of your map would help you pray accordingly.

On a local level, you could make a map of your community. On that map, you could mark all the schools and colleges in green, government buildings in brown, and the bars and adult bookstores in blue. Next, you could shade poor economic areas in purple, and stronger economic areas in red. You could highlight churches with yellow, and mark important local industries or small businesses with black. Patterns often emerge, and you'll discover ingenious ways to pray that you never would have considered before.

Using a spiritual map of the territory in which you are prayerwalking, you will be better informed about how to pray. You can make your prayer effort strategic, targeting parts of the city that have little or no Christian influence or are obvious demonic strongholds.

GRID PRAYING

In order to cover an entire neighborhood, grid praying is highly effective, particularly if you have already designed a map of that grid (a specific portion of the city or a neighborhood of the city or suburb). This type of prayerwalking consists of going into a section of town and covering it in prayer block by block. Grid praying is a great way to pray with a friend. The two of you can set out on opposite sides of the street, walking in the same direction and praying for every home, business, and church on your respective side. At the end of each block, check to make sure your friend is with you, and then continue up the next block.

Grid praying is an efficient way to bathe a city in prayer. A prayer team using this method can cover a small town in a few hours.

EIGHT PLACES YOU CAN PRAYERWALK

As you are constructing a simple spiritual map to assist you in finding the most important, or strategic, areas for prayerwalking, there are several key sites that you might consider. This list is adapted from Steve Hawthorne's list in his book entitled *Prayerwalking: Praying On Site with Insight* (Creation House).

1. The workplace.

Many people at New Life Church enjoy praying at their place of business. Sometimes they will pray over their coworkers as they go from office to office. They may meet together with other Christians at lunchtime and pray and fast through their lunches. Sometimes they walk around the building and pray during their breaks. No one suspects anything, of course, because it isn't unusual to see people taking a few moments for exercise in the middle of the day.

2. Consecrated sites.

These are sites that are set aside for spiritual purposes, such as churches. Other consecrated sites are lodges of secret societies or places where people participate in evil spiritual practices. Pray for the spirit of adoption (Rom. 8:15) and discerning of spirits (I Cor. 12:10) to fall over mosques, temples, and synagogues. Pray for an outpouring of the Holy Spirit at all places of worship so that blinders can be removed and the glorious light of the gospel will be revealed. When praying for churches, pray that the original purpose of God for that church would be fulfilled.

3. Overlook points or high places.

Most cities have high places. The Bible helps us understand that these places are important both topographically and spiritually (I Ki.11:7, 12:31; Num.33:52; II Chr. 11:15, 17:6). A few years ago we took a group of city officials to the top of Pike's Peak, the highest point overlooking Colorado Springs. They didn't fully understand the implications of what they were doing, but we instructed them on how to bless our city. They asked God to pour out His Spirit on the city and to break every curse and negative word spoken against the people of Colorado Springs.

Unfortunately, too often even Christians have cursed our cities. In prayer we must break these curses and ask God to bless our cities at these high points.

4. Sites of harm or tragedy.

Historically some of the great world atrocities were committed during the Crusades. From the 11th to 13th centuries, Christian crusaders slaughtered thousands of innocent Muslims and other unbelievers in the name of Christianity in Europe and the Middle East. Believers have recently begun to go to the countries in which these murders occurred to perform "reconcilia-tion walks," apologizing to the Islamic community for the sins of our Christian ancestors. As they have done this, the Islamic communities have opened up to the gospel. In some places, Islamic leaders have even called ahead to other mosques and towns and said, "There is a team of Christians coming to apologize for the Crusades. Open things up for them. Receive them warmly."

In America, Christians are walking along the infamous Trail of Tears and apologizing to Native Americans for our ancestors deceiving them and taking their ancestors' land. For the first time, we are experiencing a breakthrough in both of these cultures.

5. Sites of past or ongoing sin.

Adult bookstores, houses of prostitution, and bars are all places of ongoing sin. Many communities have old buildings and houses that were known for their ungodly activities. You can walk in front of these places and claim that ground for the kingdom of God.

6. Power points.

For some reason, there are places that seem to be habitations of great spiritual activity. In Colorado Springs, Garden of the Gods Park used to be known as a power point. It was home to a high degree of witchcraft and was the primary reason why Manitou Springs, a nearby community, was laden with a heavy amount of witchcraft and occult activity. Over the last few years, due to the prayer efforts of Christians all over Colorado Springs, the devil's hold over Garden of the Gods and Manitou Springs largely has been undone.

7. City gates.

Sometimes when I pray over Colorado Springs, I pray for the people who are driving or flying in and out of the city. We need to pray for people as they go to and from our cities. Pray that God will send angels to minister to people as heirs of salvation (Heb. 1:14) as they enter your city. Pray that they will have positive encounters with Christians and that they will grow hungry for the gospel as they enter your town through the various interstates, highways, county roads, and airports.

8. Land for sale.

Many intercessors enjoy driving out to land that is for sale and prayerwalking around the property, claiming it for the kingdom of God. In prayer, we take the land off of the open market in Jesus' name, and pray that only God Himself will choose the new owner of this land or home or building. Our goal is for the property in our cities to be used to advance the kingdom of God—the land on which New Life Church and the World Prayer Center stand was claimed for God years before we even considered buying it.

Remember that the property represented in all of these places belongs to the Lord, and that is why it makes sense to pray over it. The land on which your place of business is located belongs to God in the exact same way as does the land on which your church building stands. You should worship in both places, pray in both places, and love people in both places. When you pray over the people in these areas it opens the way for them to have an encounter with the Lord Jesus, to get into a life-giving church, and to fulfill the plan of God for their lives.

Chapter Three

Praying "Thy Kingdom Come"

When Jesus gave us His guidelines for prayer in the Sermon on the Mount He instructed us to pray, "Thy kingdom come. Thy will be done on earth, as it is in heaven" (Matthew 6:10, KJV). We recite these words often, knowing that heaven is the place where God's perfect will is in full expression. In heaven there is no suffering, no pain, no heartbreak, no sorrow, no aging, no hospitals, and no bad pizza. In heaven there is perfect health, harmony, peace, love, and contentment.

Today's world is a long way from heaven. As Christians we have a slice of heaven in our hearts—just enough to give us a desire for more. But most people have never known even a measure of the power or peace of God in their lives. That is why Jesus told us to pray in that way—so that Earth could be a little more like heaven.

Praying that God's kingdom come, His will be done is one of the greatest prayers we can pray as we walk our cities. When we pray this way, we are asking that God would send His Kingdom into people's lives and that His will would be increasingly established here on the earth. We are asking that things go the way He wants them to and that everyone would come into an understanding of what it means to die to themselves and live for Jesus.

FOUR POWERFUL FORCES

In order to understand how to pray for God's kingdom to come, we must gain a biblical understanding of our world. There is much confusion over why the world is the way it is. Why is there sin? Why do people suffer? Why do bad things happen to good people? Certainly these questions can be confusing, but the Bible presents a clear message about why the world works the way it does.

Our environment is influenced by four powerful forces: God's will, Satan's will, human will, and natural law. Everything that happens is a result of one of these forces. Actually, more often than not, two or more of the four forces are working in tandem with one another, but if we understand each force we'll know better how to pray.

1. God's will.

The principal force affecting the world is God's will. Again, God's will is perfectly pictured for us in heaven, which is why we pray for heaven on Earth. Sometimes God forces His perfect plan upon people, but most of the time He works gently in our lives, waiting for us to submit voluntarily to His calling. According to the Scriptures, God works in our hearts as we surrender to Him. As we respond to Him, God calls us to prayer, holy living and obedience to His commands. He wants us to be empowered by His Spirit, obedient to His Word, and free of demonic influences and bondages, and He likes to help us in all these areas.

But whether or not we respond to His help and see His will manifested, we can always understand His perfect will as revealed through the Scriptures. When we prayerwalk, we pray that God's perfect will would dominate the lives of the people in the community for which we are praying. We pray that they would respond to His will and not be overcome by the other three forces acting on their lives.

2. Satan's will.

At direct odds with God's will is the will of Satan. Satan administrates his wicked deceptions through evil spirits, or demons. Demons try to influence people to do anything other than the will of God. Their business is to lie and to deceive. They seek to promote every kind of wickedness and disaster in people's lives. The greatest bondage they establish is keeping people from finding God's perfect plan. On our prayerwalks we should exalt God's plan over the devil's—binding demonic powers and inviting the power of God into the lives of all whose paths we cross as we pray.

3. Human will.

In addition to God's will and Satan's will, people are influenced by their own personal wills. Every person is born with the choice either to go their own way or, by the drawing of the Holy Spirit, to submit to God. Most people, even Christians, live according to their own wills. They decide how to live their lives, based on what they think or feel is best. The human will quickly responds to vanity, power, control, and greed. Without restraint, the human will is wicked. Ironically, when people choose their own will over the will of God, they are actually submitting to the will of the devil. Contrary to popular opinion, they can only go two ways: they can serve God or serve the devil. We should pray that God will give people the grace they need to be drawn by God unto Himself, and submit their lives to His will rather than to their own.

4. Natural law.

The final influence on our environment is natural law. Because we understand natural law, we wear safety belts, have speed limits, build insulated homes, and brush with fluoride toothpaste. Non-spiritual people often believe that everything in life is based on natural law, which is a major error. It is equally foolish when spiritual people think that everything that happens to them is either a result of God's direct intervention or a manifestation of a demonic activity.

Neither side has a healthy understanding of the integrated roles of natural law and spiritual realities in our lives. The world often works simply according to natural law and nothing else. When God intervenes and overrides natural law, we call that a miracle. So when we are prayerwalking we ask God to supernaturally override natural law by protecting families, healing the sick, and undoing negative influences in people's lives so they can live according to God's perfect plan for them.

When we realize that our lives are influenced concurrently by God's will, Satan's will, human will, and natural law, we see the vital importance of prayer. If we want God's will to dominate over the other three competing influences in a particular situation, we must ask for "His kingdom to come, His will to be done, here on earth as it is in heaven." As this prayer is answered, God's ways will increase in the earth, people's sinfulness and Satan's manipulation will decrease, and natural law will become subject to God's will.

We all rejoice when Jesus' lordship is dominant in our lives. For all of us, though, the manifestation of His lordship is a process. In the midst of this process, when a person sees Christ's power replace demonic power, we call that deliverance. When we see God's will dominate our will, we call that being Spirit-filled. And when we experience God's grace overriding natural law, we call it a miracle. All of these wonders are enhanced and developed through prayer, and they all help manifest His Kingdom on the earth.

PRAYING THE WORD

Scripture is God-breathed. When we pray Scripture, we know that we are praying God's perfect will. To my knowledge, praying Scripture is the most effective way of interceding, because when we pray this way we are literally praying God's Spirit and truth into people's lives.

> To my knowledge, praying Scripture is the most effective way of interceding, because when we pray this way we are literally praying God's Spirit and truth into people's lives.

When I prayerwalk I use a number of Scriptures in my prayers. For years I have been praying Isaiah 11:2 over people. This verse lists the seven natures of the Spirit of God, and is included in a prophecy of the coming of the Lord Jesus (Isaiah 11-12). It reads, "The Spirit of the Lord will rest on him – the Spirit of wisdom and of understanding, the Spirit of counsel and of power, the Spirit of knowledge and of the fear of the Lord..."

When we pray this verse over people, we are praying for their specific needs to be met by these particular ministries of the Holy Spirit. Each of the following is a particular manifestation of the work of the Holy Spirit. Even though we are using different titles for each manifestation, these are all just specific descriptions of God's one Holy Spirit. It works as follows:

♦ Praying for the Spirit of God to rest on someone is asking that God's presence would inhabit their lives. We are praying that they would be surrounded by good instead of evil and that the spiritual atmosphere around them would be positive and light instead of negative and dark.

♦ The spirit of wisdom helps people to make godly choices. If the spirit of wisdom is ministering to someone, they will know the right thing to do.

♦ The spirit of understanding helps people think correctly, be discerning, and relate to others in a godly manner.

♦ The spirit of counsel helps people to receive instruction from the Lord.

♦ The spirit of power gives people the supernatural ability to live for God. It empowers them to choose God's will over their own and gives them confidence in doing ministry on His behalf.

♦ The spirit of knowledge helps people clearly see how to live for Christ and make good decisions. It gives people information and thoughts that they would not naturally have.

♦ The spirit of the fear of the Lord helps people to revere God and submit to His will. It brings an internal revelation that there is a God, that He has definite opinions, and that He will one day sit in judgment over everything and everyone.

If I were walking through a block in my city, I would use this verse of the seven-fold Spirit of God to pray specifically. Coming upon a home, I might say, "Lord, I pray that the Your Spirit would rest upon this family. I loose the spirit of understanding upon the mother in this house, and I pray that she would understand how to raise her children in godliness. I pray that the spirit of knowledge would give her fresh ideas about how to care for her family. Lord, let the spirit of counsel rest upon the dad so he would have supernatural insight about how to serve You and how to love his family. Let the spirit of the fear of the Lord dominate all the relationships in this household so that they will love, respect, and help one another..." and so on. By simply recalling Isaiah 11:2, I can pray effectively for the entire family.

Another great set of Scriptures to use on your prayerwalks is Galatians 5:22-23. This is an extremely profound and relevant Scripture to pray for people, because fruit is the natural byproduct of the presence of the Holy Spirit. The fruit are as follows:

♦ love
♦ joy

- ◆ peace
- ◆ patience
- ◆ kindness
- ◆ goodness
- ◆ faithfulness
- ◆ gentleness
- ◆ self-control

Let's say you come across a bar in your prayerwalk, and you want to pray Galatians 5 for the people in the bar. You would simply begin to list the fruit and pray that they would be manifested in each of the lives represented in the bar. Again, when you are praying for someone to exhibit the fruit of the Spirit, you are praying that the Holy Spirit would have His way in their lives and that the kingdom of God would increase.

In I Corinthians 12, Paul lists some of the gifts of the Spirit. This is another important Scripture to pray over people. In verse 7, Paul says that "to each one is given the manifestation of the Spirit for the common good." Then he offers a partial list of the gifts:

- ◆ wisdom
- ◆ knowledge
- ◆ faith
- ◆ healing
- ◆ miraculous powers
- ◆ prophecy
- ◆ the ability to distinguish between spirits
- ◆ tongues
- ◆ the interpretation of tongues

One reason I like this list is because it includes the discerning of spirits. I pray for discernment of spirits when I am praying around government buildings so that public servants, judges, juries, and others who serve us will be able to discern the difference between the truth and lies. Wisdom in discerning the difference between right and wrong, good and evil, justice and injustice is fundamental to the building and maintenance of a good society. We as Christians have an obligation to participate and pray for improvement in our cities.

Praying for people to prophesy, or speak what God is speaking, is powerful. We have several accounts in Scripture where people suddenly began to speak the perfect will of God (Numbers 11:25, I Samuel 19:24). I pray that teachers, administrators, business people, judges, city council members, and county commissioners would prophesy when answering questions or giving speeches. Prophecy is simply hearing God's still, small voice and repeating it. We all need more of that.

Praying that God would give people a gift of faith does two things. First, it may help them come to a revelation of Christ if they are not already believers. Second, faith may help someone to have the courage and perseverance to do what is right in a difficult situation. Faith causes people to put their trust in God and to experience true communion with Him.

The gifts of tongues and interpretation, as we are applying them here, can help people pray the perfect will of God and understand what they are praying. I pray this way especially when I'm praying for churches, synagogues, mosques, temples or shrines. God uses this gift to help me pray only the perfect will of God for everyone who goes to any type of worship service.

Too often we see God's kingdom, His attributes, fruit, and gifts in the context of how they operate in a church service. But I maintain that His Kingdom is not only to be manifested in church services or in the lives of believers. God wants us to pray for His kingdom to come and His will to be done in all the earth as it is in heaven. Thus, I think we ought to pray the Word over the people of our city, whether they are believers or not (a touch of heaven around them is better than no heaven at all). We have the authority, and thus the responsibility, to stand as intercessors for the people of our cities.

Other important Scripture to pray include Romans 8:15, from which we pray the spirit of adoption as a child of God, Philippians 1:9-11, and Ephesians 1:16-19. Obviously, this is not an exhaustive list of Scripture references. There are literally hundreds of Scriptures that will be valuable to you in prayerwalking. Make a list of them, commit them to memory, and go for it!

Chapter Four

Prayer
Changes
Things

In Colorado Springs, some teachers at one particular school have been praying through the school for a number of years. They walk around the school and simply pray that the ministry of the Holy Spirit would increase. Then, before and after classes, when it isn't obvious, they discretely walk the halls and pray in the classrooms.

Not long after they began doing this, people began questioning the principal, who had no idea his teachers were praying, as to why the atmosphere at that school was much more positive than at other schools. They noticed that the drug problem had decreased, that violence was less of a problem, and that the students were generally happier. Time after time, the principal would get up in the assembly and explain that their school had been given a wonderful report.

Although the principal did not realize it, the difference was not the curriculum, the funding, or the quality of the administration. Of course, those issues, properly addressed, help. But those factors were all static; just like at all the other schools. The difference was that the people of God had decided to serve this school in Jesus' name! Their prayer changed things.

PRAYER IS VITAL TO THE SPREAD OF THE GOSPEL

Billy Graham will not go into a city with a crusade until Christians have prayed over that community for an entire year. Why? Because he understands two things: (1) people cannot come to the saving knowledge of the Lord Jesus unless the Spirit of God prepares the way, and (2) one of the main tools God uses to prepare the way is the prayers of His saints.

Jesus' example shows us that it is imperative to pray for unbelievers that they may receive the gospel (John 17:20-26). We do not have the power to force people to make a decision for Christ, nor would we want to. But we as Christians do have the authority to control the spiritual environment around people and even the spiritual environment of the city at large. In order to pray effectively for God's kingdom to come into the lives of others, we need to understand **our** position in Christ. We are ambassadors for Christ—co-laborers with Him in the cause of the gospel. In the first chapter of Ephesians, Paul states at length that God has placed all things under the dominion of Christ *"for the church,* which is His body, the fullness of him who fills everything in every way" (vv. 22-23, emphasis added). We are the church. All things are under Christ's feet for all of us who are God's children. When we pray based on these facts, we exercise the awesome authority of Christ over the darkness that holds people in bondage.

> **Because of Christ's position of authority, we can enter into prayer with the bold understanding that the power of Christ that is in us is far greater than the powers of this world.**

Ephesians 1-3 highlights three foundations that are crucial to praying effectively:

1. Christ's power and authority has been given to us (Ephesians 1:19).

Paul states that God has incomparably great power for us who believe. In describing this power, Paul writes that it is "far above all rule and authority, power and dominion, and every title that can be given, not only in the present age but also in the one to come" (v. 21). Thus, in Christ we have the ability to bind evil spirits from doing their work and to loose the Spirit of God to dominate the spiritual environment (Matthew 16:19, Matthew 10:7-8). Because of Christ's position of authority, we can enter into prayer with the bold understanding that the power of Christ that is in us is far greater than the powers of this world.

2. As believers, our position is in Christ at the right hand of the Father. Christ literally shares His position with us (Ephesians 2:6).

We conclude our prayers with saying, "...in the name of Jesus" because we recognize that we pray from the position of Christ—we pray in His stead, in His nature, as His representatives. God wants us to stand as Christ's ambassadors and to proclaim His precedence over the Evil One (Satan) who is keeping the people of this world in bondage and darkness. From our position in Christ, God wants us to release His light, life, and presence.

3. We pray from heaven, not from Earth (Ephesians 3:10).

God uses the church to enforce His Word, His will, and His plan to "the rulers and authorities in the heavenly realms." In my book *Primary Purpose* (Creation House), the chapter on praying from heaven explains how we can use the authority Christ has given us as believers to negate demonic strongholds over a city. These prayers open the heavens so that people have greater freedom to make right choices when presented with the gospel.

In addition to using our position in Christ to create a more positive spiritual climate, we can also pray these five biblical guidelines for those who are unchurched:

1. Pray that the Father would draw them to Jesus (John 6:44).

Since people are totally depraved, they cannot come to Jesus without God drawing them. When we pray for the unsaved as intercessors with Christ, we are altering the spiritual dynamic surrounding them and opening the door for God to draw them in.

2. Bind the spirit that blinds their minds (2 Corinthians 4:4).

You may have experienced a situation in which an unbelieving friend simply cannot grasp the message of the gospel, even though it has been explained clearly and lovingly. The reason for this, writes Paul, is that the devil has blinded the minds of unbelievers so that the light of the gospel is hidden from them. When we pray against this blinding spirit to prevent it from its work, the Spirit of God can then open the unbelievers' eyes and give them the freedom to understand the gospel message and decide if they want to follow the Lord.

3. Loose the spirit of adoption (Romans 8:15).

It is important for us to loose the spirit of adoption upon unbelievers, for the Bible says it is by this spirit that we cry, "Abba, Father." In other words, the spirit of adoption works in us to help us to become God's children. When we have this spirit, we begin to see ourselves in the light of His fatherhood.

4. Pray that believers will cross unbelievers' paths and enter into positive relationships with them (Matthew 9:38).

It is imperative that we pray for laborers of the gospel. In other words, we must ask God to increase the number of effective missionaries, evangelists, apostles, and other workers so that the message of salvation will be lovingly, efficiently, and powerfully preached. It is important that unbelievers have positive experiences with Christians in their lives so that nothing like bitterness, resentfulness, or misunderstanding will hinder them from salvation.

5. Loose the spirit of wisdom and revelation on them so they may know God better (Ephesians 1:17).

People cannot receive the gospel unless they have some understanding of who God is and what their relationship and responsibility to Him is. The spirit of wisdom and revelation will give them that understanding.

Prayer changes things. Prayer efforts all over the world have produced real results; there is good evidence that prayer prepares people for the gospel. Every time we have gone into a foreign country and prayerwalked, that country has experienced dramatic growth in the kingdom of God within twelve months.

Here in Colorado Springs, where New Life Church joined with 70 local churches to distribute the *Jesus* film, we had a 40 percent greater response in those neighborhoods through which Christians prayerwalked before distributing them than in other neighborhoods. The act of physically getting into the streets of Colorado Springs and interceding for the lost made an objectively verifiable difference in people's openness to the gospel. There's no doubt about it: if we are faithful to pray, God's kingdom will be manifest with greater power.

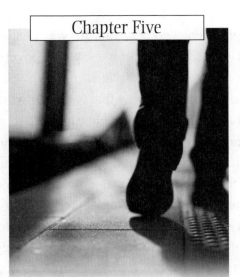

Chapter Five

Changing
the Spiritual
Atmosphere

A few years ago, some of us went up to the state capitol building to walk around and pray. It was about 9:30 at night, and we were casually dressed in blue jeans, t-shirts, and caps. At one point, one of my fellow prayerwalkers turned to me and joked, "Boy, wouldn't it be great if our governor pulled up so we could pray over him?"

A few minutes later a limousine drove up, the door opened, and out stepped our governor! He walked past us, greeted a couple of us, and continued on into the building. The capitol had been dark, and we watched as the lights came on in his office. Right then we knew that he was dealing with some important issue. So, because we saw our governor while out prayerwalking, we were motivated to pray for him for an extended period of time in a way that we never would have if we had prayed alone in our prayer closets.

If you are willing to walk your streets in prayer, you will find an endless number of things about which and people for whom to intercede. While praying alone in your room may be wonderful and effective, praying in the streets will lead you to pray in ways you would never have thought to pray otherwise. What used to be twenty minutes of struggling to concentrate could easily turn into an entire evening of exciting intercessory prayer.

Let's say you're going to prayerwalk through your own neighborhood. As you leave your house, you will immediately see your neighbors' homes. Perhaps they are your close friends, or maybe you know them on a last name basis only. Regardless of your relationship with them, seeing their homes will remind you to pray the Lord's blessings on their lives. Maybe you will remember something specific they may have told you about their lives. Perhaps their in-laws are staying with them or their oldest son is in trouble at school. Maybe six months ago someone in their family had been diagnosed with cancer. These are all things you can lift up to the Lord for them.

As you walk along, surveying the homes on the street will give you ideas about how to pray for those families. Are there toys in the yard? Pray for the parents to be godly and to raise their children honorably. Is the sound of fighting coming from within? Pray that the Lord will bring healing to relationships.

Speak blessings on the elderly couple sitting on their porch, on the single mom trying to be patient with her three-year-old, and on the young boy playing basketball in his driveway. Exalt the name of the Lord Jesus over every home, and pray that His kingdom come, and that His will be done.

Perhaps you will come across a government building, such as the county courthouse. Pray for local council members, the county commissioner, the mayor, the governor, and the presiding district attorney. Pray that the Holy Spirit would instruct them as they make executive decisions. If you come across a police station, pray the Lord's will be done

> If we are willing to take our praying to the streets, ... we will see the captives worship God in freedom, and our churches will be overflowing with people who have discovered the glorious grace of God!

in the lives of the officers and that He would protect them as they do their duty. Pray blessings on all these people as they serve your city (2 Timothy 2:1-2).

When you come to a school, spend a little time walking around the building and claiming the lives inside for Christ. Pray that the faculty would have a revelation of heaven and hell. Pray that the spirit of adoption would fall upon the students, that they would be broken enough to accept Jesus and bold enough to say "no" to the multitude of temptations that students face. Pray blessings upon the janitorial staff, the administrators, and the counselors. Claim that school for the kingdom of God.

Some of these ideas above may be things you would think about in your normal prayer times, but most of them would never come to mind unless you were out walking the streets, seeing the sights. When we're willing to get out of our homes and churches, we are more connected and passionate toward others. We can find, see, hear, and touch the lost. And God brings us opportunities to pray in ways we never imagined.

AFFECTING YOUR CITY FOR CHRIST

In 1994, a local businessman was trying to establish a pornography shop in Colorado Springs. For some reason the city government stopped him. When the newspaper asked him what the problem was, he said, "My problem is the Christians in this city. This city is under siege and you know it!"

He was right! The business owner could not have known that we actually had a banner in our church that read, "Siege this city for Me. Signed, Jesus." Somehow, that message got into the spiritual climate of our city and even the unchurched community was aware of the spiritual transition that was taking place.

A few years ago an article ran in our local paper, *The Gazette*, about a pagan who was calling for a nationwide prayer effort to channel "positive energy" into Colorado Springs. When asked by a local television station why this prayer request was necessary, he replied that he felt persecuted whenever he tried to perform his pagan rituals because the Christians in the city had been praying, which prevented his rituals from producing any spiritual response!

Both these men were correct in assuming that Christians

were to blame for the "problems" they were experiencing. Christians were not physically hindering these men from the freedom to do as they chose, but I think a Christian influence was felt due to the effects of fervent prayer. There was a definite improvement in the spiritual climate.

Even so, I did not like the fact that the unchurched community was feeling threatened by the growth of an evangelical influence. Contrary to what these men probably thought, I do not expect people who don't know the Lord to live their lives as if they were believers. We do not pray for people and offer to present the gospel to them in order to control them in any way. Rather, our intention is to serve. We want to give people the opportunity to find eternal life in Christ.

Several years ago, a group of men from our congregation took it upon themselves to pray for the people frequenting the adult bookstores in Colorado Springs. They felt that the Spirit of the Lord was calling them to pray over these places and over people with sexual addictions, so they decided to actually go to these places, park in the parking lots, and pray for those who went in and out of the shops.

On several occasions they would watch a man drive up, park his car, get out, and approach the adult bookstore. They would begin to pray, "Father, we ask that you would convict this man. Remind him of every Scripture he has ever heard. We bind the power of darkness away from him. We bind the spirits of lust and deception, and pray that You would remind him of his family. Please God, help him be faithful to his wife and children. Help him, Lord! Remind him of his mother! We loose the Spirit of God upon this man. Cause him to walk in Your ways," and so on.

I'm convinced that many of these men received more prayer walking across the parking lot of an adult bookstore than they ever had in their lives. And I guarantee that those praying in the car prayed more fervently than they ever would have in a church. Sometimes those praying would watch as the would-be bookstore patrons would pause, think to themselves, then turn around and proceed back to their cars and drive away without ever going into the bookstore.

Who knows what kind of trouble those men walked away from by responding to an improved spiritual climate around them. If the Christians had not been praying, some of those men may have continued into the bookstore and fallen into all types of sin and disgrace. But because the intercessors were there to stand in the gap, the Spirit of God was able to convict them powerfully and keep them from falling. Note that the ones praying were not concerned with picketing the shop or screaming Scripture at those who walked in. Instead, they directed their energies toward the source of the problem, which involved defeating the work of the devil in these people's lives. In doing so, they promoted the will of God and brought those for whom they were praying one step closer toward the kingdom of God.

ALTERING THE ENVIRONMENT

Every human being, whether they know it or not, is affected by a number of spiritual elements. When we pray for someone, we are directly addressing those elements and attempting to replace all that is bad with all that is good. We do not have the authority in prayer to change people's minds, but we do have the authority to interfere with the spiritual climate on their behalf so that the forces of God rather than evil forces will affect their minds.

Imagine an ordinary young man (we'll call him Max). Max is an average person living in an average town. He is an unbeliever. As such, he is still completely dominated by his sinful nature. That old sin nature can only be abolished as Max responds to the Lord of his own volition. No one has the power to change Max's mind except for Max.

Complicating matters for Max is the fact that there is demonic activity surrounding him. Spirits of despair, fear, deception, condemnation, and rebellion may be influencing Max daily. When Max sins, those spirits want to encourage him to sin more, thus creating stronger bondages to the sin patterns. If Max wants to rebel against the law, the demons will reinforce those intentions by saying, "Go ahead. No one will find out. Ignore those policemen. Just do it this once. You won't get to heaven anyway, so you might as well have fun while you are here."

Fortunately, one of Max's buddies is a Spirit-filled believer (we'll call him Joe). Joe understands that prayer is a confrontation with the devil as well as communion with Jesus. Joe also realizes that Max's sin nature is controlling Max. So instead of just trying to change Max's mind, he begins to pray for the spiritual environment surrounding Max to change.

"Lord," he says, "I ask that You would remove the spirit of rebellion from Max's life. I pray for Your Kingdom to come into his life and that he be freed from sin and condemnation in Jesus' name. I pray You would drive immorality away from Max's life. Lord, let Max experience Your light and life. Surround him with wisdom and revelation and love.

Replace the spirit of deception in his life with faith in Jesus Christ."

As Joe prays these things, he is not able to change Max's mind. He is able, however, to interfere with the spiritual climate surrounding Max. And, if there is indeed demonic activity around Max, Joe has the authority to confront those demons in the name of Jesus.

Now, because Joe has been praying for Max, Max's environment will begin to be ruled by the Spirit of God rather than the devil. As a result, when someone presents Max with the gospel, he is much more apt to believe, because his mind is not blinded by those forces that have been working in his life. What used to sound cryptic and senseless to Max will now ring with life-giving truth, for the spirit of deception has been driven out by the kingdom of God.

Isn't it wonderful that we can have confidence and hope when praying for our unsaved family and friends? It is so exhilarating to see someone who was bitter, selfish, and miserable become joyous and free when the Spirit of God moves on their life. We must continue to pray for the lost, knowing that prayer opens the way for people to come into a life-changing relationship with Christ.

PRAYER IS A MATTER OF COURAGE

Prayerwalking is simple and powerful. So what keeps people from doing it? I believe that an element of fear permeates the church today. It's as if a trembling voice cries within our hearts and our congregations, convincing us not to do anything too risky for the cause of Christ. For many Christians this cowardice, whether linked to personal sin or to the threat of embarrassment, renders many of us ineffective in the struggle for the gospel. If Christianity is dead in your community, if churches are suffering in apathy and darkness, it is largely due to this fear.

The Bible is clear concerning the consequences of fear. In Revelation 21:8, which lists those who will be thrown into the lake of burning sulfur, the first group listed is the cowardly. Additionally, Joshua 1 promotes the ideas of strength, courage, confidence, and obedience in advancing God's purpose on Earth. The biblical picture is unmistakable: fearful, spineless, faithless people cannot successfully advance the kingdom of God.

It is time for us to wholeheartedly obey the Word of God. It is time for us to regain the upper hand and help our cities. We must embrace our God-given place as ambassadors for Christ and fight for the life and health of our communities. We must encourage one another to stop cowering inside our churches and homes, frightened of what our friends and neighbors might think. We must choose to take steps to advance the kingdom of God.

You may be familiar with the story of Moses sending Caleb and the other spies to inspect the land of Canaan to see if they could capture it (Numbers 13). When the spies returned after forty days of inspection, most of them spoke fearfully of the fortified towns and the large, powerful inhabitants. Their hopes to capture the land were daunted as they trembled at the sight of the forceful people of Canaan.

Caleb, however, wasn't persuaded. He agreed that the enemy was formidable, but he was not shaken because he understood that God *had already given them the land.* Silencing the anxious cries of his fellow spies, he said to Moses, "Let us go up at once and occupy the country. We are well able to conquer it" (v. 30).

Our hearts must be like that of Caleb. We, too, have inspected our cities, and we understand that the kingdom of darkness is largely in control of people's lives. But we must also understand that the land belongs to God. When other Christians look at this intimidating situation and faint-heartedly say, "This is too much for us. Let's just put on another radio show and hope that a Christian runs for governor," our response must be, "No! Let us go up at once and occupy the country. We are well able to conquer it." We need to look the sin and pain of our cities straight in the eye and say with confidence, "We are well able to conquer it."

Never once has the kingdom of God advanced unless forceful people took decisive action against the kingdom of darkness. Our attitude must not be, "Well, I'll just try my best to love people and hope that maybe they will see Jesus." Rather, we must be like Caleb. When others are trembling in trepidation, we must rise up and say, "Give me this city. I am taking this land. I am here to dispossess sin and rebellion and take what God has promised. I am a representative of the Lord God and I am here to do harm to demonic forces. We are not going to let the children of our city be taken into violence and drugs and hatred and pornography. We are not going to let the marriages of our city crumble into easy divorce."

Our primary goal is to bring freedom to captives by the power of the gospel of Christ. We must not be distracted from that goal, and we must be bold enough to let nothing stand in our way. Now is the time for us to say, "Come on,

Holy Spirit. Move in our city in a significant way so that we can see Thy kingdom come, Thy will be done in our city, our state, and our country as it is in heaven."

Prayerwalking is not the only way for us to be courageous in advancing the gospel in our communities. However, if fear of rejection or embarrassment is what is keeping us from walking our streets in intercession, we need to find the strength to overcome our apprehension. We need to get out of our basements, and get into the streets in confidence, humility, and prayer.

"EVERY PLACE WHERE YOU SET YOUR FOOT WILL BE YOURS"

After the death of Moses, the Lord commanded Joshua to boldly enter into the land that He had promised. "I will give you every place where you set your foot," the Lord told Joshua (Joshua 1:3). Today, this is God's promise for His church. Like Joshua, we must be strong and courageous as we enter into unfamiliar territory with the plan of God on our minds and in our hearts. We must take seriously God's promise to give us all the places where we walk. As God's church and Christ's ambassadors, we have a responsibility to go out and claim the land for God's purpose.

Again, there is a special dynamic to walking your community in prayer. It wakes you up. It refreshes your relationship with God. It helps you to understand how to care for people, how to pray them into the Kingdom. It opens your eyes, and gives you a zealous, tangible compassion for the lost.

If we are willing to take our praying to the streets, we will be able to take the land for God. As we pray, we will see the manifestation of the kingdom of God in people's lives. The light of Christ will be brighter. The sick will be healed. The depressed and hurting will rejoice. Marriages will be restored. Children will honor their parents instead of rebelling, and parents will love their children instead of neglecting them. We will see the captives worship God in freedom, and our churches will be overflowing with people who have discovered the glorious grace of God!

Subject Index